IR

D1614335

True Tales of the Wild West

Fearless Scouts

Jeff Savage

Enslow Publishers, Inc.
40 Industrial Road
Box 398
Berkeley Heights, NJ 07922
USA
http://www.enslow.com

Original edition published as *Scouts of the Wild West* in 1995.

Library of Congress Cataloging-in-Publication Data

Savage, Jeff, 1961–

  Fearless scouts : true tales of the Wild West / Jeff Savage.

    p. cm. — (True tales of the Wild West)

  Rev. ed. of: Scouts of the Wild West. 1995.

  Includes bibliographical references and index.

  Summary: "Explores scouts, the men and women who opened up the West, including early
scouts like Sacagawea, other famous scouts like Kit Carson, and the maps and trails that
scouts helped create that changed the American landscape"—Provided by publisher.

  ISBN 978-0-7660-4024-3

  1. Scouting (Reconnaissance)—West (U.S.)—History—19th century—Juvenile literature. 2.
West (U.S.)—Social life and customs—Juvenile literature. I. Savage, Jeff, 1961– Scouts of
the Wild West. II. Title.

  F596.S2357 2012

  978'.01—dc23

2011028125

Paperback ISBN 978-1-4644-0032-2

ePUB ISBN 978-1-4645-0477-8

PDF ISBN 978-1-4646-0477-5

Printed in the United States of America

092011 Lake Book Manufacturing, Inc., Melrose Park, IL

10 9 8 7 6 5 4 3 2 1

To Our Readers: We have done our best to make sure all Internet addresses in this book were
active and appropriate when we went to press. However, the author and the Publisher have no
control over, and assume no liability for, the material available on those Internet sites or on other
Web sites they may link to. Any comments or suggestions can be sent by e-mail to comments@
enslow.com or to the address on the back cover.

Illustration Credits: © 2011 Clipart.com, a division of Getty Images, p. 7; Enslow
Publishers, Inc., p. 34; © Enslow Publishers, Inc. / Paul Daly, p. 1; Everett Collection, p. 40;
Library of Congress Prints and Photographs, pp. 8, 12, 14, 22, 42; Little Bighorn Battlefield
National Monument, p. 26; Mary Evans Picture Library / Everett Collection, p. 30; © North
Wind Picture Archives, p. 20; Shutterstock.com, p. 18.

Cover Illustration: © Enslow Publishers, Inc. / Paul Daly.

Contents

chapter 1

Kit and the Bear

Kit Carson raised his rifle, took careful aim, and—*bang!*—blasted a bullet right into the elk. The animal collapsed to the ground, dead on the spot. Carson was pleased to have bagged some food at last. It had been several days since he and his trapper friends had eaten meat.

Carson was a twenty-six-year-old explorer working as a scout in the Black Hills of what is now South Dakota. The year was 1835, and the land in which Carson found himself was part of the howling wilderness of the West. Only a handful of white people knew much about the land west of the Mississippi River, or about how to survive in such terrain. Kit Carson was one of them.

The trappers for whom Carson worked had been hunting for beaver pelts. It was Carson's responsibility as scout to be the eyes and ears of his group. He had to guide the trappers through rugged country, fetch food for them, and keep them from harm. What's more, there were plenty of ferocious animals prowling about, as Carson was about to discover.

Carson leaned over to inspect the dead elk. All at once, he heard a terrific roar from behind him. He snapped his head around, and there they were—two large grizzly bears, charging right at him!

Carson had already fired his gun, and he had no time to reload it. He spotted a nearby pine tree and made a run for it. The grizzlies—in hot pursuit—were at his feet when he reached the tree. He dropped his gun and leaped to the safety of a tree limb just in time. "I had to drop my gun—the bears rushing for me, I had to make all haste to ascend the tree," Carson later explained.[1]

With his gun lying on the ground at the grizzlies' feet, Carson had no choice but to sit in the tree and hope the bears would leave. One grizzly lost interest quickly, but the other stayed. It pawed at Carson, who couldn't climb any higher. To protect himself, Carson broke off a tree branch and used it to hit the bear on the snout each time it got too close. The bear snarled and growled. The sky grew dark as night arrived.

While out hunting for elk, Kit Carson was attacked by two grizzly bears. One quickly left, but Carson had to fend off the other snarling bear for hours, seeking safety in a tree.

It wasn't until midnight that the grizzly got bored and wandered away. Carson dropped down from the tree, picked up his gun, and dashed the mile back to camp.

The trappers were thrilled to see him. They had feared that he was lost, or worse, dead. Carson told them about the grizzly bears and said that he had never been "so scared in all my life."[2] With the bears still lurking, Carson didn't dare to go back for the elk. The trappers wouldn't have meat for supper again that night, but they didn't mind. Their scout was safe.

Kit Carson was a brave scout. He led many trappers and explorers through the Western frontier. This photo of Carson was taken later in his life.

Carson had always wanted to be a scout. He grew up listening to stories about Daniel Boone, a scout from Kentucky. Even before the Declaration of Independence was written in 1776, Boone was making history in America as a great explorer. He blazed a trail known as the Wilderness Road. Young Kit Carson wanted to be a frontiersman like Boone.

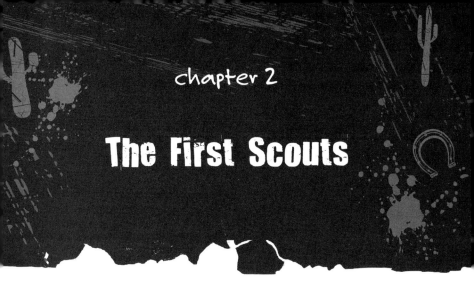

chapter 2

The First Scouts

When the first white settlers arrived in America, they met both friendly and unfriendly American Indians. Many settlers, such as the Pilgrims of Massachusetts, might not have survived without the help of American Indians. Later, in the French and Indian War, eastern American Indians took sides and served as guides for both the French and the British. The British and American troops in the Revolutionary War were led once again by American Indian scouts.

When the United States purchased Louisiana from France in 1803, the new nation nearly tripled in size. To back up its claim, the United States needed to settle the land quickly. The government encouraged people to establish homes in the frontier. At that time, however, western North America was still mostly unexplored by white settlers.

Meanwhile, the American Indians had been living on this land for thousands of years, and many of them did not welcome the westward expansion of white settlers. The American Indians wanted to keep their land, eventually fighting settlers and soldiers in hundreds of bloody skirmishes. Yet the first scouts to lead the expansion were American Indians.

Sacagawea

One of the first American expeditions through the West was aided by an American Indian—Sacagawea. Explorers Meriwether Lewis and William Clark are famous for their travels through the Pacific Northwest in 1804–1806. Their names might not be known today if not for the help of Sacagawea.

Sacagawea was a Shoshone woman who had been purchased and married by a French-Canadian trader named Toussaint Charbonneau. With Jean-Baptiste, their newborn son, Charbonneau and Sacagawea joined the Lewis and Clark expedition. Charbonneau was hired as an interpreter, and Sacagawea was hired as a guide.

The mere presence of Sacagawea and her baby saved the Lewis and Clark expedition from attack countless times. American Indians knew upon seeing a woman and a baby that the group was not a war party. Eventually, the expedition reached its goal—the Pacific Ocean.

The same year that Lewis and Clark completed their journey, explorers Zebulon Pike and Stephen H. Long began leading U.S. Army expeditions through the same wilderness that the Lewis and Clark expedition had traveled.

Early Scouting

The tales of early scouts spread through the towns of the eastern United States. People soon realized the significance of the land west of the Mississippi River and began to head west. They knew about the dangers that lurked in the vastness of the West, but they knew little about the land itself. For instance, the pioneers in the first wagon train to the West Coast in 1841 knew only that Oregon lay somewhere to the west. They did not know how long the trip would take, nor did they know whether they would survive the mountains or scorching deserts along the way. Scouts were needed more than ever.

Trappers joined American Indians in providing their services to whoever hired them. Many of them lived among the American Indians and had adapted to

White scouts and trappers often had good relationships with American Indians, who helped them learn to survive in unfamiliar territory. In this illustration, trappers sit around a campfire with American Indians.

their ways of life. The American Indians taught the trappers how to survive on their own. These skills were invaluable to the pioneers.

Though white settlers poured into the West by the thousands, many American Indians were not hostile toward them. White scouts traded, worked with, and even lived in the villages of American Indians. They became blood brothers, married American Indian women, and sometimes were declared chiefs.

To do all this, scouts had to communicate with the American Indians. There were dozens of American Indian nations, and each one had a different spoken language. It was impossible to learn all the languages, so scouts and American Indians frequently used sign language, making signals with fingers and hands.

Duties of the Scouts

Scouts were responsible for the safety of the people they were leading westward. They served as a vital resource for the survival of both explorers and pioneers. They were the eyes and ears of these groups.

Some of the things they would be called upon to do included:

◇ Keeping a sharp eye open for signs of danger.

◇ Finding the safest route and sticking to it.

◇ Finding ways to cover their tracks.

◇ Persuading expedition leaders to follow their advice.

◇ Locating food and clean water for settlers and horses.

◇ Hunting and fighting off dangerous animals.

◇ Carrying urgent messages.

◇ Translating for American Indians.

A wagon train of white settlers is headed toward California. Scouts were essential in helping settlers survive as they traveled west. Finding a safe route, locating clean water and food, and communicating with American Indians were among their many important tasks.

Scouts examined the ground and found clues that saved the people they were guiding from attack. They marked their way through barren plains. They made clever decisions about when to travel and when to hide.

Food

Food was sometimes difficult to come by. Bread, for instance, was nonexistent. Kit Carson ate bread about once a year. A scout named Jim Bridger went seven years without bread. Another scout survived for seventeen years without a single piece of bread. Fruits and vegetables were also scarce in such places as the Mojave Desert and the Rocky Mountains. The only food that almost always was available was meat, so scouts ate plenty of it, often consuming ten pounds a day.

What if there were no animals to hunt? Scouts survived as best they could. A desperate scout would cut his horse to draw blood, add water to the blood, and drink it as soup. If things got worse, he would kill the horse and eat it. When that option wasn't available, scouts would eat anything that crawled. They munched on spiders, grasshoppers, and worms. Scouts who crossed barren stretches of sand often had to devour a stew of black desert crickets. One scout even recalled plunging his arm into swarming anthills and then licking off the insects.

Major General Grenville Dodge, a chief engineer for the Union Pacific Railroad, worked with many scouts. Dodge wrote:

> Nothing escaped their vision. The dropping of a stick or breaking of a twig, the turning of the growing grass all brought knowledge to them, and they could tell who or what had done it. Their methods of hunting game were perfect and we were never out of meat. Herbs, roots, berries, bark of trees and everything that was edible they knew. They could minister to the sick, dress wounds—in fact in all my experience I never saw [them] meet any obstacle they could not overcome.[1]

chapter 3

Pioneer Scouts

S couts often rode several miles ahead of their party to ensure the safety of the route. A scout named Thomas "Broken Hand" Fitzpatrick once had a terrifying experience while he was riding alone in the Rocky Mountains. (He became known as Broken Hand after a rifle accidentally discharged and shattered his wrist.)

Broken Hand was guiding a group of men through a rugged area known as South Pass. He was a few miles ahead of the group when he came across a Gros Ventre war party. The Gros Ventre lived in what is now eastern Idaho. The warriors spotted Broken Hand on his horse, and the chase was on.

Broken Hand's horse galloped over boulders and through ravines until it could go no farther. The Gros Ventre were still right behind him. Broken Hand jumped off his horse and ran, clutching his rifle up a mountain of solid rock. He found a crack in the rock and squirmed in, then quickly covered the opening with leaves. The Gros Ventre searched along the mountainside for Broken Hand, coming within inches of him, but they could not find him. They knew that he could not go far without his horse and that eventually he would have to come out of hiding. So the Gros Ventre built a campsite at the base of the rock mountain, and they waited. Broken Hand lay still for three days and nights. He was trapped.

Broken Hand had no food or water; he knew he had to escape. On the fourth night, he decided to make a run for it. He crawled out from the crevice and crept down the mountain. Miraculously, the Gros Ventre did not hear him. He could not see in the dark. However, because he was such a good scout, he still figured out where he was. He began a long journey to Pierre's Hole, which was the original destination of his group. The next day, he arrived at the swift-flowing Snake River. To cross it, Broken Hand used a small boat that he built from tree branches. Halfway across, the boat smashed into a rock. Broken Hand managed to swim safely to the other side, but he lost his lone remaining possession—his rifle—in the river.

A view of the Rocky Mountains. Thomas "Broken Hand" Fitzpatrick was leading a group through the South Pass of the Rocky Mountains when he was attacked by a Gros Ventre war party. Broken Hand had to find a hiding place in the mountains.

For the next five days, Broken Hand staggered along toward Pierre's Hole. He stopped occasionally to rest and to dig up roots for food. His moccasins had worn off, and his feet were bloody and sore. He tore his leather hat into strips and wrapped them around his feet. At one point, he found himself cornered by a pack of hungry wolves. They charged him, and he escaped by climbing a tree. As he sat in the tree, a buffalo happened by. The buffalo was attacked by the wolves and was killed. When the wolves finally wandered away, Broken Hand dropped from the tree. He ate some raw buffalo meat, then trudged on. He went as far as he could until he collapsed from exhaustion.

When Broken Hand was found the next day by a pair of men who had been sent to look for him, he was near death. Pierre's Hole was just a few miles away. The men carried him back to camp, where he was nursed back to health. It was quite an ordeal, and Broken Hand's appearance proved it. When he first encountered the Gros Ventre war party two weeks earlier, his hair was brown. The incredible journey had turned his hair white. Broken Hand was given a new nickname—"White Hair."

No scout found any satisfaction in a wild pursuit such as this. There always was a bright side for scouts—during their wild journeys, they sometimes discovered a new trail. Getting credit for such a discovery, however, was another matter.

Elisha Stephens, Isaac Hitchcock, and Caleb Greenwood

Elisha Stephens, Isaac Hitchcock, and Caleb Greenwood were three scouts who discovered the California Trail in 1844. This trail was an old American Indian path that split off from the Oregon Trail and went southwest through the Sierra Nevada to the gold country of northern California. Stephens, Hitchcock, and Greenwood spread the word about this trail. Thousands of emigrants soon began using the route to reach the gold mines, yet these three men were barely recognized for their achievement.

Elisha Stevens, Isaac Hitchcock, and Caleb Greenwood discovered the California Trail. But the three scouts received little credit for their discovery. In this illustration, a group of explorers are climbing a mountain pass on the California Trail.

Jesse Applegate and Moses Harris

Jesse Applegate and Moses Harris led a scouting party that forged a new route from the California Trail to southern Oregon. The route broke from the trail at the Humboldt River in Utah and wound northwest through the Cascade Mountains. For some reason, Harris gained no fame for his part in creating the new route. It became known only as Applegate Trail.

Scouting for the Army Corps

In 1836, the government created a small army unit known as the Corps of Topographical Engineers. The men were responsible for mapping the vast western territory. Eventually, every mountain and river were accounted for.

The corps inspected mountain passes to find routes where wagon trains could travel and railroad tracks could be laid. The corps searched for areas containing supplies of water, food, and grasses in which to build forts. For a quarter of a century, these army engineers studied millions of square miles of land. They couldn't have done it without the help of scouts.

Antoine Leroux

Among the most famous scouts for the corps was Antoine Leroux. He helped guide teams of engineers along the cliffs of the southern Rockies and through the deserts of the Southwest.

The Corps of Topographical Engineers, an army unit created by the U.S. government, was responsible for mapping out the western territory. The corps could not have achieved their accomplishment without the help of scouts. This photo shows a group of topographical engineers in Yorktown, Virginia, during the Civil War.

Leroux's first assignment in 1846 was to lead a corps group commanded by Captain Philip Cooke. The corps was looking for a wagon route from Santa Fe, New Mexico, to San Diego, near the Pacific Ocean. The problem was that the Rocky Mountains were in the way. Leroux said he could find another way to get to San Diego, and so they set off.

Leroux wanted the corps to go south along the Rio Grande for 230 miles, then southwest into Mexico for another 160 miles to get through the mountains at Guadalupe Pass. Captain Cooke agreed to this plan, at first.

Leroux traveled more than fifty miles ahead of the corps as he searched for water and for ground smooth enough for wagons to roll across. He would communicate with the corps by using smoke signals or by leaving notes attached to trees.

The corps traveled for more than a month, and Captain Cooke was getting more frustrated each day. He was in too much of a hurry. He didn't like the idea of going around the mountains. Why not just cut through them?

Leroux waited for the corps on the trail one day. He had good news: Guadalupe Pass was just one more day away. Captain Cooke didn't care. He was fed up. He demanded that the corps head west—now! There was nothing Leroux could say that would change the captain's mind.

The men scaled up and over a mountain, hiked through a ravine, then went along steep cliffs until they could go no farther. They were stuck. The only way that they could escape was by lowering the wagons by rope from jagged rocks. Several wagons were destroyed, and Cooke's men were exhausted by the time they got across the mountain. From there, they pressed on through the desert until they reached San Diego.

Thousands of settlers and miners used this route to get to California for years afterward. Of course, they wisely traveled the extra day to cross the mountains at Guadalupe Pass. The trail was named after Captain Cooke, even though it was his scout, Antoine Leroux, who discovered the route.

Scouts in the American Indian Wars

Another purpose of the army's Corps of Topographical Engineers was to locate American Indians and to inform the U.S. Cavalry of their whereabouts. The cavalry would then violently force the American Indians off their land. For years, scouts had led groups of white men *away* from American Indians. Now their job was to lead them *to* the American Indians.

Several army scouts were noted for their skill at finding American Indians. Among them were Will Comstock, Lonesome Charley Reynolds, Luther "Yellowstone" Kelly, Frank Grouard, and Johnnie Bruguier.

Will Comstock

The business of guiding the army through the West was dangerous, yet scouts were paid little for their efforts. Will Comstock once led an army of men through a blizzard for two weeks. On the day he got the group to safety, he was fired.

However, Comstock was so knowledgeable that the army kept coming back to him. He worked most often with Lieutenant Colonel George Custer, who later gained fame in the Battle of the Little Bighorn. "He is a valuable man," the colonel wrote about Comstock, "and I am constantly learning valuable information from him regarding the Indians, their habits, etc."[1] There was nothing more to learn from Comstock after August 16, 1868. That is the date on which he was killed—shot from his saddle by Cheyenne warriors.

Lonesome Charley

Lonesome Charley Reynolds was once hired by the army to carry a report more than one hundred miles between two forts in the Black Hills. The danger was that the Dakota Territory was the home of the Sioux, who were being attacked by the army. Reynolds volunteered for the job. He traveled by night, and he hid with his horse in bushes during the day. The Sioux often passed so close that he could hear them talking, but they never caught him. He reached the fort safely, and he presented his report to the army commander.

Reynolds became so skilled at hunting antelope, elk, and deer for the army that American Indians nicknamed him "Lucky Man." But he wasn't so lucky on June 25, 1876, when he guided Custer's Seventh

Lonesome Charley Reynolds was killed at the Battle of the Little Bighorn. This painting by Richard Lorentz depicts the victory of the Sioux and Cheyenne warriors at the battle.

Cavalry to the Little Bighorn River for a massive battle with Sioux and Cheyenne warriors led by Crazy Horse and Sitting Bull. Reynolds was among the hundreds of men killed; he was shot through the heart. The battle became known as the Battle of the Little Bighorn.

American Indians as Army Scouts

Colonel John Gibbon of the U.S. Seventh Infantry wrote of the American Indian scout: "He knows every path, every pass in the mountains and every waterhole as thoroughly as the antelope or other wild animals which range through it. He knows exactly where he can go and where he cannot."[2]

American Indians even scouted for the U.S. Army. Many American Indians began to realize that the coming of the white settlers would not stop. Their land would never be the same again. Instead of fighting against this invasion, some American Indians switched sides and began fighting for the U.S. government. And most were pleased to receive the pay of $13 a month. By 1866, about one thousand American Indians were serving as scouts. Some of the greatest American Indian scouts were Bloody Knife and a Crow scout named Curley, both of whom worked for Custer and the Apache Kid.

The Apache Kid

The Apache Kid helped the U.S. Army in a number of battles against the Apache leader Geronimo. The Kid was so respected by the army that he was elevated to the rank of first sergeant. After many years of loyal service, however, the Kid suddenly became a man hunted by the army.

The Kid discovered that his father had been murdered. He wanted revenge. The Kid tracked down and killed one of his father's murderers. The Kid was later captured and sentenced to seven years in prison. He and his comrades, however, escaped on their way to jail. For years, the Kid was hunted by his former coworkers but was never found.

chapter 5

Jim Bridger and Kit Carson

K it Carson was thought by many to be the greatest scout ever. Others say the supreme scout was Jim Bridger. Both men contributed mightily to the exploration of the West, and both had plenty of memorable experiences along the way.

Jim Bridger

Bridger had learned the terrain of much of the West as a fur trapper and guide. He led large groups of trapping parties across the Great Plains, through the Rocky Mountains and the Sierra Nevada Mountains, and into California. When he came across lost travelers, he used a piece of charcoal to draw a map of the region on a buffalo skin, and he would give it to the travelers to use as a guide. Sometimes, he would pour handfuls of sand on a blanket to form mountains, using his

Jim Bridger was the first white American to discover the Great Salt Lake in Utah.

fingertips to draw rivers. He seemed to know almost every hill and hollow throughout the West.

Bridger was so admired that some people gave him affectionate nicknames. A Bible-reading mountain man named Jedediah Smith said that Bridger reminded him of the archangel Gabriel, so Smith and his friends called him "Old Gabs." For parties and other special occasions, Bridger would wear a colorful blue robe made for him by his American Indian wife, so the American Indians called him "Blanket Chief."

Bridger liked to sit with friends around the campfire and tell them stories of his exciting life as a scout. Some of the stories were far-fetched, while others were strange but true. Two of the mysterious places he liked to tell about were the river that flowed so swiftly that it got hot at the bottom and the river that flowed in two opposite directions at once.

Both of these wonders were real. One was the Firehole River, in what is today Yellowstone National Park. There, an underground hot spring heats the water. The other was Two Ocean Creek in the Grand Teton Mountains of Wyoming. Many rivers split into two branches along a line known as the Continental Divide. At this line, one branch of Two Ocean Creek began to flow eastward down the mountain, while the other flowed westward down the other side.

Bridger also could tell stories to the American Indians, using sign language. He would point and gesture silently as his audience stared at his hands. They would occasionally gasp with fear or laugh hysterically.

Bridger didn't always get along with American Indians, however. While he was scouting with a group of trappers in 1832, Bridger's party came across a band of Blackfoot. One of the Blackfoot rode forward with a peace pipe, and Bridger came out to meet him halfway. It was a trick; the Blackfoot grabbed Bridger's rifle and conked him over the head with it.

A battle broke out that didn't end until nightfall. Nine Blackfoot and three trappers were killed. Bridger was shot with arrows twice in one shoulder. His friends were able to remove one of the arrows, but they could only snap off the shaft of the other, leaving the arrowhead lodged in Bridger's shoulder. Bridger didn't have the second arrow removed until he saw a doctor three years later.

Bridger demonstrated his keen eyesight one time while he was leading an army expedition. He pointed out a thin column of smoke that was rising above some distant hills. The army general and his men could not see the smoke, even with the use of binoculars. Other scouts rode in later and told of an American Indian village in the precise spot that Bridger had pointed out.

Kit Carson

Kit Carson, like Jim Bridger, learned American Indian ways at a young age. Kit lived in a log cabin in Missouri with his parents and four older brothers. By the time Kit was ten years old, he had learned to hunt with a rifle. He was friendly with American Indians, and he soon learned to speak their language. When Kit was twelve, he was given his first horse. He taught himself to shoot from the saddle, even while he was hanging under the horse. Finally, at the age of eighteen, Kit Carson joined a group of settlers bound for New Mexico. He had become a frontiersman.

Over the next decade, Carson learned the ways of a scout. He could survive in the wilderness, and he could communicate with American Indians through sign language. Most important, he could "read sign," which meant that he could determine the general activity of the area by finding clues. Carson could

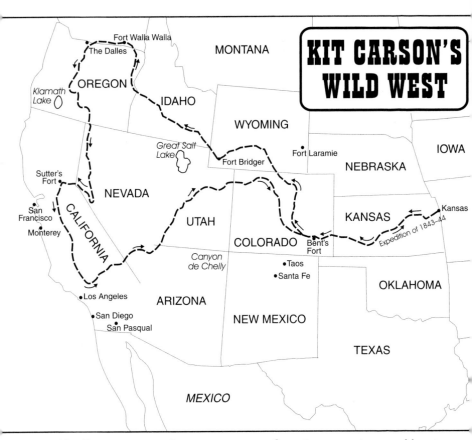

KIT CARSON'S WILD WEST

Kit Carson covered a vast amount of territory as a scout. He scouted for many groups and explorers, most notably John Charles Frémont. He and Frémont opened up new areas of the West to settlement. This map shows some of Carson's journeys.

examine streams, grasses, sand, or even tree bark and figure out who had been there and when.

As gifted a scout as Carson was, he probably never would have become famous if it weren't for an explorer named John Charles Frémont. Likewise, Frémont never would have accomplished all he did without his main scout, Carson. Together they forged new trails through the Wild West, opening up the wilderness for thousands of settlers.

The two men met by chance on a train in 1842. Carson was hired at a salary of one hundred dollars per month to guide Frémont's expedition through what is now South Dakota. Carson displayed courage and skill, and soon he became Frémont's permanent scout.

In 1844, Carson was guiding Frémont's expedition through the barren Mojave Desert when they came across two wounded Mexicans. The Mexicans told of an attack by thirty Paiute who had murdered the rest of their family and had stolen their horses.

With another scout named Alexis Godey, Carson volunteered to go after the Paiute. Carson expected several more men in the expedition to volunteer as well. None did, so Carson and Godey went alone. They traveled all night and found the Paiute camp at dawn. They crept close to the camp until the Paiute spotted them at the last instant. Carson and Godey shot off their rifles, and two Paiute fell dead. The rest of the Paiute figured that there were plenty more white men ready to attack. Two men wouldn't dare attack so many. The Paiute quickly fled.

When Carson and Godey returned to camp, Frémont was astounded. He later wrote: "Two men in a savage desert pursue day and night an unknown body of Indians . . . attack them on sight, without counting numbers . . . and defeat them in an instant . . . and for what? To punish the robbers of the desert and avenge the wrongs of Mexicans."[1]

Frémont failed to realize that Carson attacked the Paiute to scare them. Carson hoped to discourage them from attacking his own party. The plan worked.

For the next several years, Carson led expeditions through the West. An army lieutenant who traveled with Carson wrote: "Carson, while traveling, scarcely spoke; his keen eye was continually examining the country. A braver man than Kit perhaps never lived, in fact I doubt if he knew what fear was."[2]

chapter 6

The End of the Scout

Two later scouts who achieved an even greater and more long-lasting fame were the two Bills: Buffalo Bill Cody and Wild Bill Hickok. Both were known throughout the Wild West by white settlers and American Indians alike.

Cody was leading fifteen Fifth Cavalry soldiers one day when he spotted a group of Cheyenne coming up the trail. Cody signaled for the soldiers to hide in the weeds. As the Cheyenne approached, a shot rang out, and the fight was on. Three Cheyenne were immediately killed. The rest quickly escaped. The soldiers figured that the battle was over. All at once, the Cheyenne, who were riding away, turned around and attacked. In the midst of the fighting, the chief yelled out, "I know you, Pa-ho-has-ka! Come and fight with me!"[1] The chief was yelling to Buffalo Bill Cody. Pa-ho-has-ka meant "Long-Yellow Hair."

Buffalo Bill accepted the chief's challenge. He killed the chief's horse by shooting it with his rifle. Then his own horse stepped in a hole and fell. Now the two combatants stood face-to-face about twenty feet apart. They both fired at the same instant. The chief's bullet zipped past Bill's ear, and Bill's shot hit the chief in the chest. The chief fell to the ground, and Bill finished him off with a knife. Bill would remember the bloody scene for the rest of his life.

Bill became a buffalo hunter in 1860 at the age of fourteen. He provided food for construction crews of the Kansas Pacific Railroad. He delivered so many buffalo carcasses to the crew that they called him "Buffalo Bill."

Later that year, Bill became the youngest of eighty riders hired to carry the mail for the new Pony Express. Most of all, Bill was a scout. He worked for many years as a guide for the U.S. Army. Bill loved scouting so much that he named his only son Kit Carson Cody, in honor of the legendary scout.

Buffalo Bill was the chief of scouts for the Fifth Cavalry, and he was joined in 1868 by another crafty scout whose nickname was Wild Bill Hickok. The two

Bills were similar in many ways. Both wore their hair down to their shoulders, both were expert marksmen, and both knew the rugged terrain of the West as well as anyone.

Cody and Hickok worked side by side for the Fifth Cavalry until Hickok was attacked. He was scouting alone when he came across several Cheyenne and got into a running fight. A warrior got close enough to shove a spear through Hickok's thigh. When Cody found him the next morning, Hickok was near death. Dragging himself along the trail, he used the spear as a crutch. Cody brought his friend to an army surgeon, who saved his life and his leg.

Hickok moved to Kansas, where he served as sheriff of Hays City and later as marshal of Abilene. Cody also quit the scouting business and headed east. Neither man really wanted to stop working as a scout. The truth was that there just wasn't much use for scouts anymore.

Easterners predicted at the start of the nineteenth century that it would take five hundred years to settle the West; but they were wrong. The West was exploding with growth, and the land was no longer a mystery. This meant the end for the scout.

Wild Bill Hickok was a scout, lawman, marksman, and card player. This photo was taken of him in 1871.

As the 1800s wore on, trails once known only to American Indians were becoming more and more familiar to new settlers from the East. Precise maps were being drawn and guidebooks written. Mountains and streams were counted and mapped. The Wild West was being documented:

◇ When the Civil War broke out, armies began marching across America, carefully marking trails as they went.

◇ Thousands of miners scoured hills and hollows across the vast land in search of silver and gold. As it was important to establish ownership of claims, these areas were accurately mapped.

◇ Railroad tracks were laid west clear to California. For those with money, traveling in wagon trains was no longer necessary.

◇ Telegraph lines were crisscrossed through the West like an enormous cobweb. Information passed more quickly from coast to coast.

◇ American Indian territory shrank as settlers pushed west. Attacking war parties were no longer a risk in many areas. By 1890, the American Indian wars were over.

Buffalo Bill Cody established a Wild West show that he toured across America and Europe. Wild Bill Hickok often joined him as an actor in the show. This poster advertises Buffalo Bill's Wild West show in 1899. Although the Wild West show could never match the excitement of Buffalo Bill's life as a scout, it gave thousands of people a taste of the Wild West.

As the nineteenth century came to a close, scouts continued to travel into the far reaches of the West, but for new reasons. Instead of guiding trappers, pioneers, or armies into unknown lands, scouts led sightseeing groups, hunting parties, and wealthy tourists who wanted a taste of the Wild West. Sometimes, dime novelists and photographers went along to record the trips as scouts told tales of their earlier exploits.

Buffalo Bill Cody was a master among tour guides. He found another occupation when his true scouting days came to an end. Because most Easterners were unable or unwilling to travel west, Cody brought the Wild West to them. Cody became an actor in Wild West shows held in outdoor arenas throughout the East. He portrayed himself as a courageous scout who roamed the land. Wild Bill Hickok joined his friend as an actor in these shows, and the two Bills starred together as scouts.

Their friendship ended in 1876, when Hickok was murdered while he was playing cards in a saloon. Wild Bill allegedly was holding a pair of aces and eights when the cards spilled from his hands. Ever since, the combination has been known as the Dead Man's Hand.

Buffalo Bill was crushed by his friend's death, but he continued his acting career. For the next decade, Cody portrayed the life of the scout—drawing maps, foraging for food, hunting game, inspecting the ground for clues, battling American Indians, and guiding expeditions across the rugged land. It was all very exciting to his audiences. It could never be as exciting as it was to the scouts themselves, the men who blazed trails through the forbidding wilderness—the real scouts of the Wild West.

Chapter Notes

Chapter 1. Kit and the Bear

1. Harvey Lewis Carter, *"Dear Old Kit"* (Norman, Okla.: University of Oklahoma Press, 1968), p. 60.

2. Ibid., p. 61.

Chapter 2. The First Scouts

1. Keith Wheeler, *The Scouts* (Alexandria, Va.: Time-Life Books, 1978), p. 15.

Chapter 4. Scouting for the Army Corps

1. Keith Wheeler, *The Scouts* (Alexandria, Va.: Time-Life Books, 1978), p. 88.

2. Phillip H. Stevens, *Search Out the Land* (Chicago: Rand McNally & Company, 1969), p. 103.

Chapter 5. Jim Bridger and Kit Carson

1. Keith Wheeler, *The Scouts* (Alexandria, Va.: Time-Life Books, 1978), p. 26.

2. Ibid., p. 28.

Chapter 6. The End of the Scout

1. Phillip H. Stevens, *Search Out the Land* (Chicago: Rand McNally & Company, 1969), p. 98.

Glossary

California Trail—The trail pioneers used to get to California. It followed the same route as the Oregon Trail before breaking off near Fort Hall (Idaho) and heading southwest to Sacramento.

cavalry—An army unit of soldiers mounted on horseback.

corps—A small army unit.

emigrants—People who leave their country or their home and travel to another place to live.

frontiersman—In the Wild West, a person who has lived on the frontier and learned how to survive in the wilderness.

Oregon Trail—The trail pioneers took to get to Oregon. Most pioneers left from Independence, Missouri, heading northwest over the Great Plains. The trail crossed the Rockies at South Pass and continued northwest to the Willamette Valley.

ravine—A steep-sided valley.

reading signs—To examine streams, grasses, footprints, and other signs in order to figure out who has recently been in a certain area.

scout—A person who stays ahead of a traveling group to make sure all is safe and clear ahead. He also looks out for food, water, and shelter for the group.

topographical—Relating to land surfaces and to prominent features, such as mountains, valleys, and rivers.

Further Reading

Berne, Emma Carlson. *Sacagawea: Crossing the Continent With Lewis & Clark.* New York: Sterling, 2010.

Calvert, Patricia. *Kit Carson: He Led the Way.* New York: Marshall Cavendish Benchmark, 2007.

Palmer, Rosemary G. *Jim Bridger: Trapper, Trader, and Guide.* Minneapolis, Minn.: Compass Point Books, 2007.

Roza, Greg. *Westward Expansion.* New York: Gareth Stevens Publishing, 2011.

Sheinkin, Steve. *Which Way to the Wild West?: Everything Your Schoolbooks Didn't Tell You About America's Westward Expansion.* New York: Roaring Brook Press, 2009.

Internet Addresses

Legends of America: Explorers, Trappers, and Traders
<http://www.legendsofamerica.com/we-explorerindex.html>

National Geographic: Lewis & Clark
<http://www.nationalgeographic.com/lewisandclark/>

PBS: New Perspectives on the West
<http://www.pbs.org/weta/thewest/>

Index